Learning Lenses: Lesson Observation Guide

Chris Quigley

Published by Chris Quigley Education Limited

First published September 2012

CONTENTS

Introduction

Lenses sharpen our focus and provide clarity. Learning lenses sharpen our focus on learning. This guide is aimed at school leaders who wish to improve their focus on how pupils achieve and the reasons for their achievement. The guide takes the user through a step by step process which focuses on the seven most important aspects of teaching, which we refer to as lenses. By using the seven lenses, leaders may identify strengths and weaknesses in teaching and, in doing so, improve the quality of teaching. This version of the guide aligns its judgements with the Ofsted framework of September 2012 for schools in England.

The guide aims to make clear the distinction between monitoring and evaluation, to provide details of what should be monitored and evaluated and the process for doing this. it also offers advice on collating the information from lesson observations to help with action planning and self-evaluation.

The final section of the book provides staff training activities. They may be used to develop the main ideas within this guide. Links to video clips are included to provide opportunities for practising observation skills.

Section 1: Why observe Lessons?

Section 1: Why observe lessons?

The 3 main reasons for observing lessons:

1. To find out more about pupils' achievement:
2. To help find out why achievement is as it is:
3. To discover how to improve achievement:

To find out more about pupils' achievement

Data on pupils' achievement is only one part of a complicated jigsaw puzzle. By observing lessons it is possible to see progress in individual lessons, and in pupils' books, thus going beyond the limited information contained in the data. It is also possible to speak to pupils about aspects of their learning that are not always apparent from looking at their books, for example whether they have an in-depth understanding of knowledge and skills.

To help find out why achievement is as it is

Whilst data and lesson observations give us a clear picture of pupils' achievement it is also important to know why achievement is as it is. Through a process of evaluation, it is possible to look at the teaching provided and judge which aspects of it impact positively on achievement and which require improvement.

To discover how to improve achievement

In discovering why achievement is as it is, the strengths and weaknesses of teaching become clearer. In discovering the positive aspects of teaching, leaders may spread the effective practice to other areas.

1 Finding out more about pupils' achievement:

Achievement

Attainment and progress relative to starting points.

Finding out about achievement means looking in three main areas:

- data on attainment
- data on progress
- lesson observations, including book scrutiny, discussions with pupils and teachers.

During lesson observations it is important to describe the attainment and progress observed in that lesson and over time as seen in books and in discussion with pupils.

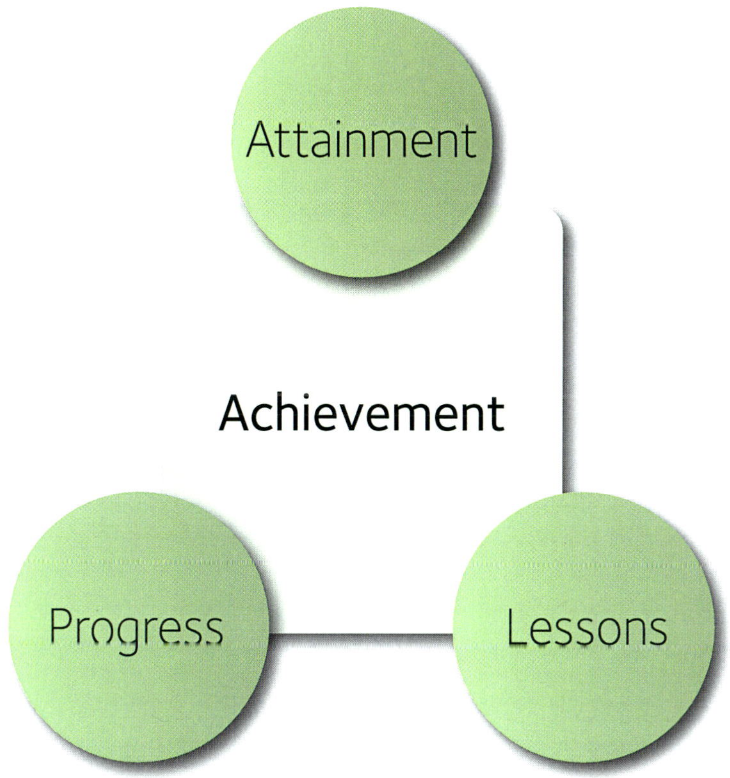

Achievement is the aspect of a lesson that should be **monitored**

Monitoring is a process of finding out. The main reason for observing lessons is to find out more about achievement for different groups of pupils. This will add to the picture data gives, and will provide more clarity about achievement. Another area that should be monitored is pupils' **spiritual, moral, social and cultural (SMSC) development**. This guide covers SMSC in section 2 as part of the attitudes lens.

Section 1: Why observe lessons?

1 Finding out more about pupils' achievement:

Achievement

Attainment and progress relative to starting points.

Finding out about achievement means looking in three main areas:

- data on attainment
- data on progress
- lesson observations, including book scrutiny, discussions with pupils and teachers.

During lesson observations it is important to describe the attainment and progress observed in that lesson and over time as seen in books and in discussion with pupils.

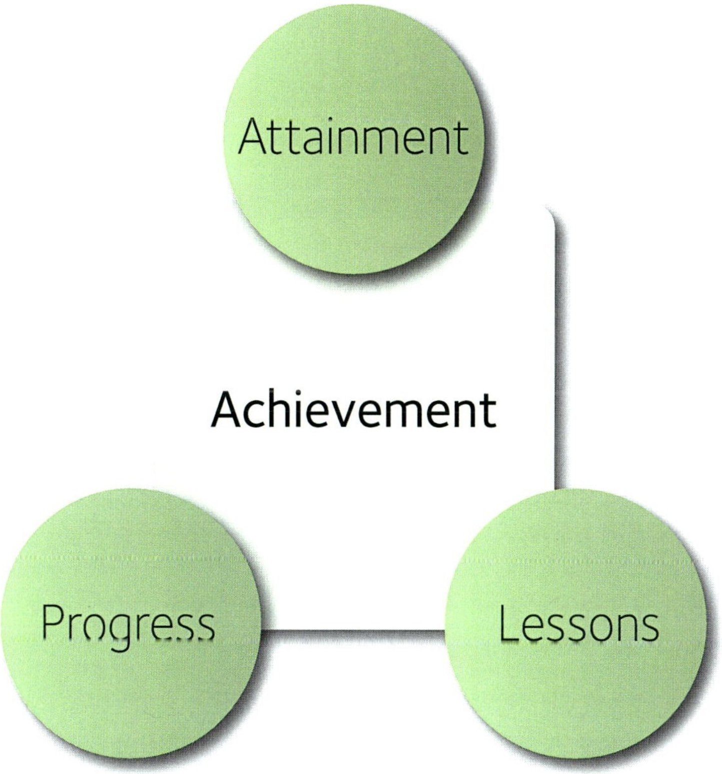

Achievement is the aspect of a lesson that should be **monitored**

Monitoring is a process of finding out. The main reason for observing lessons is to find out more about achievement for different groups of pupils. This will add to the picture data gives, and will provide more clarity about achievement. Another area that should be monitored is pupils' **spiritual, moral, social and cultural (SMSC) development**. This guide covers SMSC in section 2 as part of the attitudes lens.

2 To find out out why achievement is as it is

Whilst finding out more about the achievement of pupils, it is also possible to look at the aspects of teaching that are positively influencing progress and the areas that may need improvement.

Instead of describing the teaching methods, it is important to evaluate them in relation to their impact on progress for pupils.

It is very important to keep an open mind whilst observing teaching and not to expect any particular method. Instead, evaluate the methods used in terms of their effectiveness for that particular group of pupils.

Monitoring

Finding out about achievement and describing it in terms of the attainment and progress observed in data, lessons, discussions and books

Evaluation

Explaining why achievement is as it is by looking at the effectiveness of teaching over time

'Teaching' not 'Lessons'

Instead of trying to assign a grade to a lesson, try to look beyond this one-off situation. A lesson only gives one example of effectiveness. Alongside books, data and pupil and staff discussions, lesson observations become another piece of information in helping to explain why achievement is as it is. Ofsted grade descriptors refer to the quality of teaching and should not be used to grade lessons.

3 To discover how to improve achievement

School leaders must manage the quality of teaching so as to improve achievement. This means that a systematic approach to evaluating the quality of teaching is required.

The learning lenses approach to evaluating teaching provides seven lenses which represent the key areas affecting progress.

This guide will show you how these key areas may be used to collate strengths and weaknesses in teaching. The benefit of this is that after a round of lesson observations, conclusions may be drawn and action taken.

Monitoring

Evaluation

Action

Actions: individual and school

When identifying actions it is important to decide which actions involve individuals and which involve the whole teaching staff. Actions may include the strongest teachers working with those who require improvement. It is important to note if any actions are required in order to meet the **teacher standards** (applicable for teachers in England, as updated by the Department for Education, September 2012).

Section 2: What to look for - using learning lenses

Section 2: What to look for - using learning lenses

The seven learning lenses

Progress The most important measure of teaching is its impact on progress. The best progress is highly visible, measurable, rapid and sustained across all subjects. This lens gives the final check as to whether the efforts of teaching bring benefits in learning.

The other six lenses are all factors that affect progress. The progress lens needs, therefore, to be used in conjunction with all of the other lenses. Each lens will be explored in relation to how it promotes and helps to reveal progress.

Assessment Whilst it is possible to make progress in almost anything, the assessment lens helps teachers to plan for progress for individuals in the right things, to the right, challenging standard. This lens concentrates mostly on lesson planning and it's importance in focusing lessons on individual needs.

Checking The checking lens helps teachers to focus on the signs of progress during lessons. By continually checking on progress, teachers can maximise it and reshape their teaching as required.

Marking Progress is affected by the quality and frequency of feedback. Consistency of quality feedback helps pupils to know what they have done well and helps them to improve.

Teaching The methods that teachers use to promote progress for individuals are almost unlimited in number. This lens helps leaders to evaluate the effectiveness of the teaching methods used in maximising progress for all.

Basic skills Best thought of as the 'silent objective' of every lesson, the basic skills lens helps leaders to evaluate opportunities for developing reading, communication and mathematics in all lessons.

Attitudes The attitudes lens helps teachers to focus on the learning skills and behaviours of pupils. This lens helps leaders to identify how the traits of a competent learner are developed, including pupils' spiritual, moral, social and cultural development (SMSC).

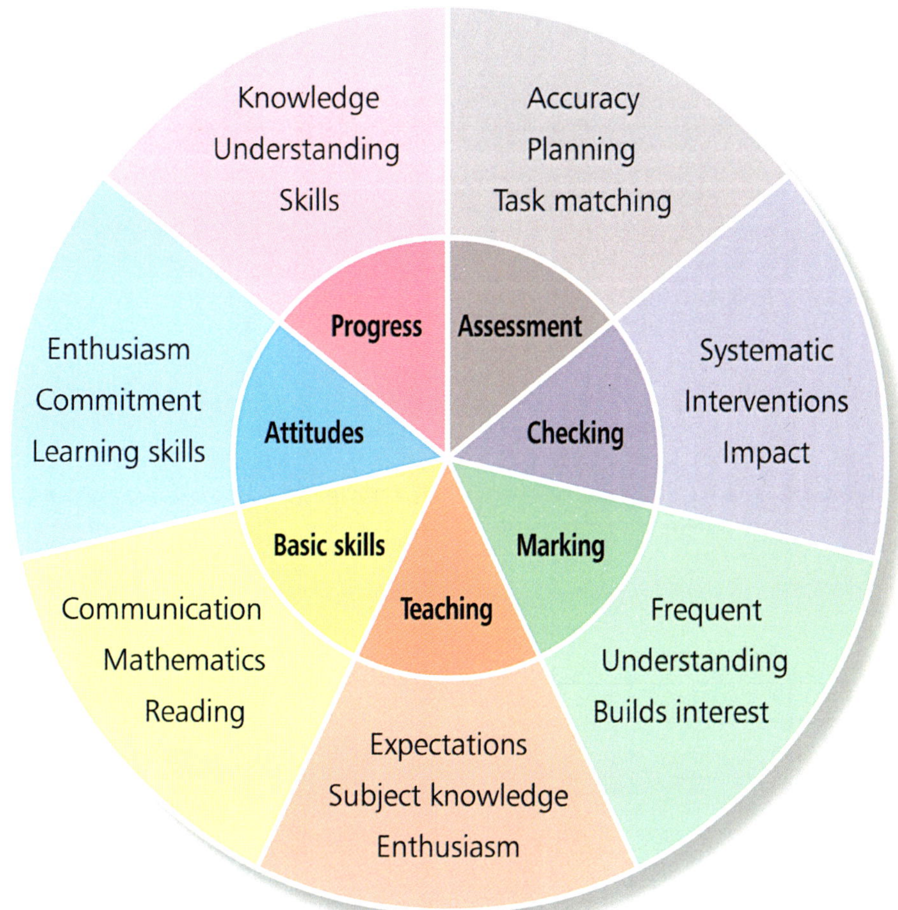

Making judgements

	Outstanding	Good	Improvement Required	Inadequate
Progress	Much of the teaching in all key stages and most subjects is outstanding and never less than consistently good. As a result, almost all pupils currently on roll in the school, including disabled pupils, those who have special educational needs and those for whom the pupil premium provides support, are making rapid and sustained progress.	Teaching in most subjects, including English and mathematics, is usually good, with examples of some outstanding teaching. As a result, most pupils and groups currently on roll in the school, including disabled pupils, those who have special educational needs and those for whom the pupil premium provides support make good progress and achieve well over time.	Teaching requires improvement as it is not good.	As a result of weak teaching over time, pupils or particular groups of pupils including disabled pupils, those who have special educational needs, and those for whom the pupil premium provides support, are making inadequate progress.
Assessment	All teachers have consistently high expectations of all pupils. They plan and teach lessons that enable pupils to learn exceptionally well across the curriculum.	Teachers have high expectations. They plan and teach lessons that deepen pupils' knowledge, skills and understanding and enable them to develop a range of skills across the curriculum.		Teachers do not have sufficiently high expectations and teaching over time fails to engage or interest particular groups of pupils, including disabled pupils and those who have special educational needs.
Checking	Teachers systematically and effectively check pupils' understanding throughout lessons, anticipating where they may need to intervene and doing so with notable impact on the quality of learning.	Teachers listen to, carefully observe and skillfully question pupils during lessons in order to reshape tasks and explanations to improve learning.		NA
Marking	Consistently high quality marking and constructive feedback from teachers ensures that pupils make rapid progress.	Teachers assess pupils' learning and progress regularly and accurately. They ensure that pupils know how well they have done and what they need to do to improve.		NA
Teaching methods	Teachers use well-judged and often inspirational teaching strategies, including setting appropriate homework that, together with sharply focused and timely support and intervention, match individual needs accurately. Consequently, pupils learn exceptionally well across the curriculum.	Effective teaching strategies, including setting appropriate homework and appropriately targeted support and intervention are matched to most pupils' individual needs, including the most and least able, so that pupils learn well in lessons.		Learning activities are not sufficiently well matched to the needs of pupils.
Basics skills	The teaching of reading, writing, communication and mathematics is highly effective and cohesively planned and implemented across the curriculum.	Reading, writing and mathematics are taught effectively.		Pupils cannot communicate, read or write, apply mathematics as well as they should.
Attitudes	Teachers and other adults generate high levels of engagement and commitment to learning across the whole school.	Teachers and other adults create a positive climate for learning in their lessons and pupils are interested and engaged.		NA

These descriptors are based on the Ofsted framework grade descriptors for the quality of teaching, September 2012.

Ofsted judgements

Remember that these descriptors do not describe the quality of individual lessons. They describe the quality of teaching as a whole, taking account of evidence over time. While they include some characteristics of individual lessons, they are not designed to be used to judge individual lessons.

Section 2: What to look for - using learning lenses

Progress and assessment

OUTSTANDING

- Clear and highly focused objectives based on thorough assessment
- Visible progress that is rapid
- Excellent pupil productivity
- Highly tuned differentiation that challenges and supports all pupils.

GOOD

- Clear objectives
- Visible progress that is good
- Good pupil productivity
- Effective differentiation.

IMPROVEMENT REQUIRED

- Objectives not always clear
- Coverage rather than progress is the main focus of planning
- High on teacher input
- Little pupil productivity
- Limited differentiation
- Not enough progress in lesson to secure progress over time.

Spotting progress

	Non-recorded work	Recorded work
Progress indicators	• Pupils' questions (verbal and non-verbal*) • Vocabulary used by pupils • Pupils' response to teacher questions • Pupils' ability to generate ideas • Pupils' predictions • Pupils' ability to reflect on actions taken • Engagement in task • Time spent on task • Work rate during tasks • Completion of task * Non-verbal questions are common in most lessons. They are the questions an observer may 'see' by watching the actions of pupils. They may, for example explore an object or turn to a page of a textbook. They are often asking questions without realising it.	• The attainment displayed* in terms of levels or standards • The quantity of work completed in the time available • Improvements made as a result of feedback • Progress made from initial part of the lesson to the final part * Remember to describe what you see in terms of attainment, linking it to a level or standard.

Progress and checking

OUTSTANDING

- Excellent, systematic and accurate checking of progress in all subjects
- Focused and timely interventions show a notable impact on progress
- Individual and group discussions are led by expertly framed questions or activities that give the teacher a deep insight into pupils' understanding without putting on hold the progress of others
- Excellent and notable impact on pupil progress.

GOOD

- A good level of checking of individuals' progress in most subjects
- Timely interventions improve progress
- Individuals or groups are the focus for checking and so progress is not hindered for any pupils
- Some effective methods shown over time
- Good impact on pupil progress.

IMPROVEMENT REQUIRED

- Some checking of progress in lessons.
- Usually reliant on whole class methods that may put on hold the progress of some or many pupils
- Little information gained from checking methods
- Reshaping of teaching has little impact on progress.

Progress and marking

OUTSTANDING

- Almost all pupils know what they have done well and the reasons why it is good
- Excellent advice in almost all subjects helps pupils to make rapid progress
- Pupils are inspired to act on the feedback and as a result are motivated to make improvements.

GOOD

- Marking gives pupils a good indication of what they have done well in most subjects
- Advice is useful and relevant and helps pupils to understand how to improve their work
- Pupils act on their feedback and as a result make good, visible signs of progress.

IMPROVEMENT REQUIRED

- Marking highlights strengths but is not always specific enough to help improve progress
- Teachers give advice but it is not always as relevant as it could be
- Few signs of visible progress emerge as a result of marking, no matter how detailed or consistent
- Advice may be good in some subjects but it is not widespread across most.

Progress and teaching

OUTSTANDING

- A wide range of often inspirational teaching methods leads to highly motivated and enthusiastic pupils who make rapid progress
- High levels of pupil productivity maximises the time for learning
- Progress is highly visible due to the excellent tasks given, that expertly match the objective
- Every opportunity is used to reinforce basic skills.

GOOD

- A good range of teaching methods is used in most subjects
- Pupils quickly engage and remain engaged throughout lessons
- Progress is visibly good for almost all pupils
- A good level of pupil productivity can be seen as a result of the effective teaching methods used
- Basic skills are used well across the curriculum.

IMPROVEMENT REQUIRED

- Methods are usually limited to whole class delivery
- Introductions are lengthy and disengage some pupils
- A narrow range of methods leads to pupils making less than good progress
- Low pupil productivity in lessons
- Missed opportunities for using basic skills.

Progress and basic skills

OUTSTANDING

- Every opportunity is taken to use basic skills across the curriculum
- Pupils are fluent in a wide range of basic skills. They demonstrate an excellent standard across the curriculum
- High quality communication, including formal speaking to an audience, is a common feature of lessons over time.

GOOD

- Most opportunities are taken to use basic skills in most subjects
- Pupils show good levels of competence in basic skills in most subjects
- Most pupils are confident in their communication with others, including verbal and written forms of communication.

IMPROVEMENT REQUIRED

- Teachers often read to pupils, rather than pupils reading for themselves
- Little use of phonics other than in taught session in KS1
- Some maths skills used across the curriculum, but many missed opportunities
- Some communication, including speaking or writing to an audience, but not to a good level.

Progress and attitudes

OUTSTANDING

- Excellent attitudes are a feature of almost all lessons. Pupils have an in-depth understanding of the attitudes they need to be successful learners
- High levels of engagement and productivity are shown by almost all pupils
- Pupils are at ease working in a range of situations and often take the initiative to act without teacher direction
- SMSC development is excellent.

GOOD

- Good attitudes are seen in most subjects because of a consistent approach to their development
- Pupils are engaged in learning and teachers enthuse them
- Pupils show resilience and determination in challenging activities
- Most pupils work independently or collaboratively, as required
- Pupils demonstrate a good level of SMSC development.

IMPROVEMENT REQUIRED

- Attitudes to learning are promoted inconsistently. Although there may be some good examples, pupils do not develop good attitudes over time
- Teaching does not enthuse pupils and engagement levels are too variable
- Pupils are reliant on adult support during challenging activities
- Many missed opportunities to develop pupils' SMSC development.

What is meant by attitudes to learning?

These 'Secrets of Success' may help you to define attitudes to learning. They are taken from a Chris Quigley Education teaching pack of the same title.

1

2

3

4

Section 3: The process and documentation

Section 3: The process and documentation

The context of lessons

What is meant by context?
The context of a lesson refers to its place within a sequence of lessons and within the overall picture of achievement as shown in other indicators (such as data).

Why is context important?
Understanding the wider context of achievement helps to us to look at lessons in a way that describes achievement and explains the reasons for it. Recognising the place of a lesson within a sequence ensures that we understand what the teacher is attempting to do and can better evaluate their success.

An example of a context statement
This is the second lesson in a series of five about fractions. Building on previous learning of denominators and numerators, the pupils will learn how to add fractions, recognising when the sum of fractions makes more than one. They will also learn to represent this.

Focusing observation to explain achievement

Why focus observations?
Analysis of data or other indicators may give some cause for concern, in which case focusing lesson observations on issues will help to explain why they exist. Issues provide a starting point but the focus for observation may change as the lesson progresses. Remember that a lesson is only a snapshot, so try to assess whether any issues are present over time.

Examples of ways in which lessons may be focused

- *Books show little recorded work.* Is pupil productivity high enough in lessons?
- *Few high attaining pupils.* Is enough emphasis placed on deepening pupils' understanding? or Is assessment used to challenge pupils well?
- *Progress seems slow.* Is the quality of feedback and marking helping pupils to progress?
- *Boys' attainment in writing is lower than girls'.* Does the teacher use appropriate teaching methods to engage both boys and girls?

Conducting lesson observations

Be descriptive of progress

It is important to quantify the progress seen for different groups of pupils. As you will see from the judgements page (page 9), Ofsted make particular note of disabled pupils, pupils who have special educational needs and pupils for whom the pupil premium provides support. Not all of these pupils are represented in each class, but if any differences are noted in data progress measures then lesson observations may be used to find out why this is.

Be evaluative of provision

Evaluation attempts to find effectiveness. Effectiveness of lessons means the extent to which teaching impacts upon pupils' progress, and over time, their achievement. Be very careful not to describe provision, or to expect any particular methods to be used. Instead look for the effectiveness of any methods used. An exercise on pages 29-30 shows the difference between describing and evaluating methods.

Useful evaluative phrases

The following phrases may be useful in linking teaching to its impact on learning:

- because of...
- as a result of...
- the impact of this was...
- this led to...
- following this...
- this resulted in...
- consequently...
- the outcome was...

Documenting your findings

Date:	Teacher:	Year:	Observer:	Subject/Area
Context:				

	Strengths	Areas for improvement	Agreed Action
Progress			
Assessment			
Checking			
Marking			
Teaching			
Basics skills			
Attitudes			

Example observation

Date: 11th July 2012 Teacher: Mrs Miggins Year: 4 Observer: Mr Darling Subject/Area: Mathematics

Context: This is a lesson reinforcing essential number knowledge. Teacher's assessment shows that although recall of tables is good, pupils still struggle to recall rapidly the 7 and 8 x tables. Data shows rapid progress for pupils in this class. Attainment is above the expected level according to teacher assessments.

	Strengths	Areas for improvement	Agreed Action
Progress	Excellent progress made in recalling multiplication facts (7 and 8) and using them in practical contexts. Strong evidence of Level 3. Most able pupils stretched by using associated division facts. SEND pupils independent but challenged well. As a result, excellent progress in acquiring knowledge of 7&8 x table. Excellent productivity throughout due to clarity of objective and well matched activities.	Some initial slower progress for one group of pupils due to checking methods.	Explore ways to put in place early progress checks, especially for the most able pupils.
Assessment	Accurate assessment used to plan differentiated work based on those who already knew but could not apply and those still acquiring knowledge. Accurate National Curriculum level pitch and suitable challenge for most able. Good task matching.		Agreed to work with Year 5 teacher, who finds assessment in mathematics difficult without testing pupils.
Checking	In discussion with pupils, they said they knew what they had done well and why this was. This is due to the teacher and assistant giving clear feedback. Whilst all made improvements as a result of feedback, one or two were not challenged by it.	One or two pupils were not challenged to improve beyond the expectations of the lesson. They had time and scope to do this.	Identify next steps for those pupils who exceed expectations so as to maximise progress. Do this at the planning stage.
Marking	Systematic checking throughout lesson, apart from one group in early part of lesson. Checking did not put on hold the learning of others.	Progress for around 5 pupils was initially limited due to lack of early checking. Teaching assistant slow to move from target group to check on progress of these 5 pupils.	Training for teaching assistant in checking techniques: in-house next Wednesday.
Teaching	Pupils were working productively within minutes of the lesson starting. Techniques such as 'sort it' helped pupils to work collaboratively, deciding on criteria for themselves. The lesson was punctuated by many different and highly appropriate activities.		
Basic Skills	Excellent emphasis on pupils reading questions for themselves. Excellent use of previously learned knowledge and high expectation of recalling number facts.		
Attitudes	Excellent focus on concentration and work ethic. Activities encouraged pupils to use imagination. Feedback helped pupils to develop the motivation to improve. Excellent use of collaboration. Behaviour was exemplary.		Work with neighbouring school to share our effective practice in shaping positive attitudes: longer term project, beginning September.

Collating findings

Summary of strengths and weaknesses

Key: S= Strengths   I= Areas for Improvement

	Teacher 1	Teacher 2	Teacher 3	Teacher 4	Teacher 5	Teacher 6	Teacher 7	Teacher 8	Teacher 9	Teacher 10	Teacher 11
Progress											
Assessment											
Checking											
Marking											
Teaching											
Basic Skills											
Attitudes											

Giving feedback

Tip: Begin discussions about lessons with two questions:

- Who do you think made the best progress and why?
- Who do you think did not make as good progress and why was that?

DISCUSS STRENGTHS

- Keep the discussion focussed on progress.
- Where was progress best seen and why was that?
- Be specific, with examples of the progress seen.

DISCUSS POINTS FOR IMPROVEMENT

- Be specific.
- Discuss the areas in which progress was limited and for whom.
- Focus on how the improvements discussed will impact upon progress. Again, try to be as specific as possible.

AGREE ACTION

- Try to be as specific as possible, noting when actions will take place.
- Agree the support or training that will be given.
- Remember that actions may involve using strengths to help other staff in the school or other local schools.

Book scrutiny

National Curriculum standard?	Evidence of progress being made?	Fluency of basic skills?
Evidence of effective feedback that improves learning?	Evidence of any self-evaluation that develops understanding?	A suitable level of pupils' productivity?
Suitable work that is based on assessment (including suitable differentiation)?	Balance of knowledge, skills and understanding?	Evidence of pupils developing resilience?
Clarity of learning intentions and activities matched to those intentions?	Any school issues that are being tackled?	A high level of challenge and relentless consistency with standards?

Lesson observations provide a good opportunity to look at progress over time, as well as in that particular lesson.

This list provides a starting point for looking for progress and achievement in pupils' books.

Section 4: Staff training activities

The difference between monitoring and evaluation

What is monitoring?	What is evaluation?

Give examples of the things that should be monitored during a lesson observation	Give examples of the things that should be evaluated during a lesson observation

Refer to **Section 1** for guidance on this activity.

Observation notes: descriptive or evaluative?

Observation notes should be descriptive of progress and evaluative of provision that affects progress. They should look at the progress made, in which areas, the reasons for it and the action that would improve progress.

Date: 11th July 2012 Teacher: Mrs Miggins Year: 4 Observer: Mr Darling Subject/Area: Mathematics

Context: This is a lesson reinforcing essential number knowledge. Teacher's assessment shows that although recall of tables is good, pupils still struggle to recall rapidly the 7 and 8 x tables. Data shows rapid progress for pupils in this class. Attainment is above the expected level according to teacher assessments.

	Strengths	Areas for improvement	Agreed Action
Progress	Excellent progress made in recalling multiplication facts (7 and 8) and using them in practical contexts. Strong evidence of Level 3. Most able pupils stretched by using associated division facts. SEND pupils independent but challenged well. As a result, excellent progress in acquiring knowledge of 7&8 x table. Excellent productivity throughout due to clarity of objective and well matched activities.	Some initial slower progress for one group of pupils due to checking methods.	Explore ways to put in place early progress checks, especially for the most able pupils.
Assessment	Accurate assessment used to plan differentiated work based on those who already knew but could not apply and those still acquiring knowledge.. Accurate National Curriculum level pitch and suitable challenge for most able. Good task matching.		Agreed to work with Year 5 teacher, who finds assessment in mathematics difficult without testing pupils.
Checking	In discussion with pupils, they said they knew what they had done well and why this was. This is due to the teacher and assistant giving clear feedback. Whilst all made improvements as a result of feedback, one or two were not challenged by it.	One or two pupils were not challenged to improve beyond the expectations of the lesson. They had time and scope to do this.	Identify next steps for those pupils who exceed expectations so as to maximise progress. Do this at the planning stage.
Marking	Systematic checking throughout lesson, apart from one group in early part of lesson. Checking did not put on hold the learning of others.	Progress for around 5 pupils was initially limited due to lack of early checking. Teaching assistant slow to move from target group to check on progress of these 5 pupils.	Training for teaching assistant in checking techniques:- in-house next Wednesday.
Teaching	Pupils were working productively within minutes of the lesson starting. Techniques such as 'sort it' helped pupils to work collaboratively, deciding on criteria for themselves. The lesson was punctuated by many different and highly appropriate activities.		
Basic Skills	Excellent emphasis on pupils reading questions for themselves. Excellent use of previously learned knowledge and high expectation of recalling number facts.		
Attitudes	Excellent focus on concentration and work ethic. Activities encouraged pupils to use imagination. Feedback helped pupils to develop the motivation to improve. Excellent use of collaboration. Behaviour was exemplary.		Work with neighbouring school to share our effective practice in shaping positive attitudes: longer term project, beginning September.

Observation notes: descriptive or evaluative?

Does this observation focus on progress and the reasons for it?

Date: 11th July 2012 Teacher: Mrs Miggins Year: 4 Observer: Mr Melchet Subject/Area: Topic

Context: This is a topic lesson about rivers.

	Strengths	Areas for improvement	Agreed action
Progress	The objective of the lesson was to write a report about rivers. Pupils were shown the learning objective and they were asked to generate success criteria. Following this, pupils used whiteboards to think of ideas to write about. They then filled in a writing frame showing their ideas about rivers. They made good progress.	The interactive whiteboard was not used.	Make fuller use of technology in learning.
Assessment	The teacher assesses pupils termly and keeps accurate records of levels and sub levels. This is then fed into our database and monitored by the Year group leaders. This forms the basis for pupil progress meetings, which are held every term.		
Checking	Plenary sessions are used to find out if pupils feel confident about their leaning. The used 'thumbs up' to self assess.	Plenary session was rather short.	Give more time for the plenary, allowing pupils to share their learning.
Marking	Marking follows the school policy. Much marking is verbal and so there is no written evidence in some lessons.	Try to indicate that verbal feedback has been given by writing VF on pupils' books.	Agreed that the VF system would be used.
Teaching	The teacher used good methods to establish what all pupils must, should and could do. Talking partners were used well. Whiteboards were used well.	More use could have been made of the interactive whiteboard in the introduction.	
Basic Skills	Pupils used talking partners to discuss their ideas.		
Attitudes	Pupils displayed very good attitudes to learning. They sat still, listened and showed good manners.		

Notes on the observations on pages 29 and 30

Observation 1	Observation 2
These observation notes give a clear description of progress. We know that pupils are reinforcing learning of the 7 and 8 times tables. We know why the teacher has chosen this as it is in the context statement. This shows a good use of assessment in planning lessons. We also know that this is pitched at Level 3 of the National Curriculum, which is appropriate for Year 4. The factors explaining progress are clearly given and so we have a good understanding of what was done well to promote progress and what could have been improved.	In contrast to the first example, this is a weak observation that does not focus on progress. It is highly descriptive of activities and is vague in describing the progress of pupils in terms of the knowledge, skills or understanding that they acquired, and the National Curriculum standard. Although it asserts that the pupils made good progress, the reader is left wondering in what. The points for improvement tend to focus particulary on methods of working rather than in identifying how progress could be improved. Comments about marking and assessment described procedures rather than provide an explanation for progress.

Video links

Teachers TV

Following the closure of Teachers TV, the Department for Education has signed distribution agreements so that the programmes in the archives are available to watch on-line.

Watch Teachers TV programmes by following the links below. This will take you to a distributor's website where you will be able to stream the programmes free of charge:

Distributor	Website
Phoenix TTV Limited	www.teachersmedia.co.uk/
Axis 12 Limited	www.teachfind.com/
Creative Education	www.creativeeducation.co.uk/videos/
Promethean Planet	www.prometheanplanet.com/PDTV
TSL Education Ltd	www.tes.co.uk/video
Alexander Street Press	www.edtv.alexanderstreet.com
viewmy.tv Limited	www.viewmy.tv
Andrew Bethell Associates Ltd	www.proteachersvideo.com
National STEM Centre	www.nationalstemcentre.org.uk/teacherstv
Laser Learning Ltd	www.laserlearning.tv
RAISEonline.Training	www.eyfsonline.org
Teach Pro Limited	www.schoolsworld.tv

SEARCH TIP: look for the 'UNCUT' series, which shows full lessons. They may be used to practise observation skills.

Use this sheet to help practise observation skills

Date:	Teacher: Year:	Observer:	Subject/Area
Context:			
	Strengths	Areas for improvement	Agreed Action
Progress			
Assessment			
Checking			
Marking			
Teaching			
Basic Skills			
Attitudes			